Growing Up Black in America

After the American Civil War,
in 1863,
black people in America
were supposed to be free.

Now they could live
in all parts of America.

In the north,
they were treated far better
than in the south.

There were laws in the south,
made by white people,
to segregate black from white.

In some places
it was against the law
for blacks and whites
to play cards together.

Ma Sch ng

Published in association with The Basic Skills Agency

Hodder & Stoughton

A MEMBER

When Martin Luther King died,
on 4th April 1968,
he was only 39.

He had been the youngest person ever
to win the Nobel Peace Prize
in 1964.

Without him,
the fight for equal rights
for black Americans
might never have happened.

Black Americans
might never have won
the freedoms they have today.

Martin Luther King is remembered
as one of America's greatest men.

His birthday
is now a holiday in America.

Even if black people grew rich,
they could never live like white Americans.
Martin Luther King
was born in the south of the USA
in 1929.

As a boy he knew what the words
"Whites Only" meant.

That meant that he could not use
the same toilet, park, cinema, or library
as white people.

It meant that his family
had to live in an area
for black people only.

He knew this was not fair.

Martin went to a college for black students.
He was so clever,
he went when he was 15,
3 years before the other students.

He studied divinity.
He wanted to be a minister of the church,
like his father.

Later Martin became a doctor of divinity.

At college Martin read about
an Indian man called Gandhi.

Gandhi helped Martin to see
how black Americans should protest
and fight for their rights,
but they should not use violence.

While Martin was at college,
he met a music student
called Coretta.
They married in 1953.

Then Martin and Coretta
went back to the south
to live and work.

They knew they were going back
to segregation.
But the south was their home.

Martin got his first job
as a church minister
in Alabama.

Fighting Back

In Alabama,
segregation was very strict.

On the buses,
all the drivers were white.
Black people had to sit at the back.

One day in 1955
a black woman called Rosa Parks
sat in a seat saved for white people.

The driver told her to move
but she did not.

Rosa was arrested.

This made black people very angry.

There was a boycott
of the buses for a year,
until the bus company gave in,
and black people could sit
on any seat on the buses.

Martin Luther King
was in charge of the boycott.

Martin and Rosa Parks
were the first black people
to get on a bus after the boycott.

Fame

This made Martin more famous,
but he was also more hated.

He got 30 hate letters a day,
and his house was bombed.

Martin had beaten the bus company,
but the violence still did not stop.

Many black people
were taken from buses
and beaten up.

Now that Martin Luther King was famous,
people all over America
wanted to hear him speak.

He gave up his full-time job,
and worked part-time as a minister.
This meant he could give his life
to speaking and protesting
for equal rights.

In 1960 he helped some students.

They could not get food
in a bus station cafe,
because they were black.

So they just sat in the cafe
day after day to protest.

Martin and the students were arrested.
He got 4 months hard labour.
John F Kennedy
helped to get Martin out of jail.

The protest went on.

White racists got very angry –
they beat up the students
and set fire to buses.

One day a mob set fire to a church
full of black people.
Martin got out just in time.

The press saw what happened
and soon the world began to take notice.

America had to begin
to change its laws.

Next the protestors went to Birmingham, Alabama
where segregation was the worst in America.

Lots of children joined Martin to march.
Firemen turned powerful water hoses on them,
then they set dogs on them.

Again, the press saw all this,
and the press told the world.

The violence in Birmingham, Alabama
made ordinary people
all over America
care about black people's rights.

Martin Luther King's Dream

Martin Luther King planned a march
to Washington in 1963.
This was 100 years
after the end of slavery in America.

Martin hoped that 100,000 people
would march with him.
In fact, 250,000 came.

He told the people
"We seek the freedom in 1963
promised us in 1863."

He said "I have a dream
that one day
sons of slaves and sons of slave owners
will be able to sit down together
at the table of brotherhood."

He ended with the words of a song:
"Free at last, free at last.
Thank God Almighty,
we are free at last."

Martin Luther King
made black and white people
feel united.

He hoped that everyone in America
would change.

He wanted to end poverty and war.

He began to work
not just for black people's rights,
but for whites as well,
poor workers and people without work.

Then the President,
John F Kennedy,
was shot and killed
in Dallas, Texas.

Martin felt sure
that this would happen to him as well.

Martin's Death

Martin Luther King
went to Memphis in April, 1968
to help some workers
who were on strike.

He went out on his hotel balcony
to get some air.
He was shot
by a man named James Earl Ray
from a building over the road.

He was taken to hospital,
but one hour later he was dead.

James Earl Ray ran away to England.
He was arrested in 1968
and sent back to the USA for trial.

Ray was a white racist
who was paid to murder King.
He never told who had hired him.

Martin Luther King's death
sent a shock wave
across America.
There were many riots,
and many people were killed.

Over 100,000 people
went to his funeral in Alabama.

They saw his coffin pulled to church
on the back of a mule cart.
This reminded people
of their beginnings,
and so did the words
on his gravestone:

"Free at last, free at last.
Thank God Almighty,
I'm free at last."